POEMS
for
PAULA

BOOKS BY FREDERICK MORGAN

POETRY

Poems for Paula, 1995
Poems: New and Selected, 1987
Eleven Poems, 1983
Northbook, 1982
Refractions, 1981
Seven Poems by Mallarmé—with images by Christopher Wilmarth, 1981
The River, 1980
Death Mother and Other Poems, 1979
Poems of the Two Worlds, 1977
A Book of Change, 1972

PROSE

The Fountain and Other Fables, 1985
The Tarot of Cornelius Agrippa, 1978

EDITOR

The Modern Image, 1965
The Hudson Review Anthology, 1961

POEMS

for

PAULA

Frederick Morgan

STORY LINE PRESS

Published by: Story Line Press, Inc.
Three Oaks Farm
Brownsville, OR 97327

This publication was made possible thanks in part to the generous
support of the Nicholas Roerich Museum, the Andrew W. Mellon
Foundation, the National Endowment for the Arts and our indi-
vidual contributors.

Cover design by Chiquita Babb

Library of Congress Cataloging-in-Publication Data

Morgan, Frederick, 1922-
Poems for Paula / Frederick Morgan.
p. cm.
ISBN 1-885266-18-9 (cloth)—ISBN 1-885266-14-6 (paper)
1. Love poetry, American. I. Title.
PS3563.0830595 1995
811'.54—dc20   95-36173
CIP

Paula's Book

TABLE OF CONTENTS

"In time all things are seeking completion,
but in *Now* all things are complete."

WORDS

How shall I say it, dear Paula?
Words may not meet the occasion.
They tend to stray off and lose contact
while love, year by year, builds in silence.

Words are like travelers, troubled
by multiple schemes and arrangements,
sometimes harassed beyond measure,
not certain they'll find satisfaction—

yet all the while trusting that somehow
they'll glean from the zest and disorder
a larger, untrammeled awareness
of what it must mean to be home.

I   THE RIVER

THE RIVER

Nous nous réveillons tous au même endroit du rêve...

1

A fresh June morning
        your dress flung across the chair-back
and birds awakening,
released from the book of night.

Here it is, the Day
        like none other from world's beginning
and all we have is in it:
I read you again and again.

2

The sun tells stories
        to the restless river
as the trees listen in.

The river is resistless—
but the trees recall the rain's
lisping insistent voice
urgent at the back of our minds
while the sun tells his stories
(familiar, widely applauded)
to the river of every day.

3

Two bodies in the river,
yours and mine, moving,
a midday swim. The sun
is sultry and relaxed.

Have I taken hold of your hand then?
Is there such sweet ease between us?

It's as though the river sums it all
in our minds and its own.

4

Now you are holding a book:
intelligence there with passion
surviving the individual brain and hand—

and when you speak of it tellingly
as we walk beneath the trees
        a living ghost stirs
in the world where all our thoughts are trees and rivers.

5

Decisions of afternoon: as,
to swim once again in the river
before the day turns dark? or
to read from a book of adventure—
of the kind refused by the crowd?

Whichever, it will be private,
unhandled by the human
except as what is human
may also be river and sun.

6

As the sun dims we begin to think
        of evenings that may have passed by
in the world only the trees know.

Only they know it because
        it's a world deprived of vision
and metaphysical striving,

a voiceless world of dense fabrics.
        You and I holding hands
touch on one corner of it.

7

Sleeping, we boarded a boat
that went drifting through our heads
down dark reflective aisles of
summertime water.

The bitterns and Spanish moss:
a Carolina dream.
Uneasy voices called out, too,
beyond the vegetable islets.

Floating, we were hand in hand,
and when our bed returned
it was as though the book had opened
to our reflective eyes.

8

A voice spoke in the night
        while the stars moved slowly
within our dreaming heads.

Not in ancient thunder, not
in the still small voice of the Lord,
but with something like
the rain's persistent utterance...

Insatiable rain!
        Our bodies clasped and clasped.
The weak stars winked out.

        9

Morning. A river view
calls out to us obscurely:
you are your naked body, crossing
whitely the open room.

Sunlight tips the trees
as if to say, A beginning.
No more is to be said.

The book lies on the bedside table:
once, it contained the night.

II MAINE

AT THE QUARRY

We have acquaintances
      up at the quarry.
A lettuce-green frog balances in the shaded corner
nose and eyes peering up from the shallows,
a water-boatman with scarlet head
glides along the watertop (he doesn't like my feet),
dragonflies in tandem hover and glisten,
a chipping sparrow rustles in the low laurel-bush
—there he goes with his *click click click*

as in the great midst we swim alone,
      naked and serene.

AT THE BEACH

The worm beneath the grass
tingles against moist roots,
the yellow jacket drills
deep into pulpy fruit:
a day of rippling airs
and golden undertones—
barefoot we wander down the beach
culling its whitest stones.

THE WAVE

Nothing is better than seaweed on rocks
and barnacles that scrape
and the harsh rub of granite
and the wind from the south bringing salt

except the sight of you naked—
Venus of every day—
arms lifted, balancing lightly
as you enter the naked wave.

THE HUMMINGBIRD

This quick one likes to tilt his spear
into each gold and crimson cup
and out again, then whir away
across our garden at midday—
soon to return, and dip and hover,
tasting his favorites once more.

Through the long honeysuckle days
of warm July he'll keep this up.
He starts at dawn. We lie adrowse
in our big bed and hear him come,
mingling his low and vibrant hum
with the soft droning of the bees—

until, one day, he'll disappear
and stay away until next year.
We have no notion where he goes.
Some day, too, he'll die, and drop
small and stiff to the ground, and rot.
Meanwhile, these hours are his.

NORTH SEDGWICK

In the deep afternoon
       August shade
at the edge of shimmering
       asphalt, three
Indian children are sitting.

Micmacs from Canada
       down for the
blueberries, they have brilliant
       muskrat eyes,
inquiring feminine faces.

In a moment we have
       driven past,
retaining though the imprint:
       T-shirts' pale
lavender, deep blue dungarees.

AUGUST

1

Cicada, harvest-fly,
you come out in the days of the dog:
your males emit the vibrant hum
of timelessness in August fields
now as in those boyhood years
when I believed time had no end.

Imagos imbibe sap of trees;
nymphs live in soil, suck sap from roots,
after seventeen secret years
assume their brief maturity.

2

Ninety degrees of August heat—
the sultriest spell in many a day!
Naked we skirt the beach's edge,
adorn ourselves with seaweed wreaths
and laugh and splash, as though at play—

then ease out through the gentle surge
to cool our bodies in the bay.

3

Via lactea, luminous belt of light
  "composed of countless worlds",
your changeless passage calms the ardent night.

Future, present, past are intertwined
within that vast unknowing mind—
yes, in your solemn circuit of a quarter-billion years
  (one round of the celestial sphere)
you justify this mortal August night.

NIGHTWATCHERS

We hear them at first dawn, a small golden ringing that comes as from many miles away, distorted by distance... Or from the innermost coilings of our own ears... And laughter, that begins and ends with the sound of wind passing through leafy branches. Were they in our rooms watching us while we slept? Or amusing themselves in the moonlight of our quiet furniture?

Mysterious tunings and tinklings! Do they have bells, musical instruments? Or do they summon up these sounds from powers that rest within ourselves? It is, in any case, a music to which no meaning may be assigned.

Yet it tempts us, with a suggestion of departures. From our silent rooms, in which (if we could but observe them at a time when they were totally unobserved) faint traces of movement might perhaps be detected; from our sleeping bodies (are we inside or outside them when they sleep?), out of whose webwork odd anomalies have been known to emerge; and from the specified, given world—as when a woman steps away from a mirror and her reflection disappears.

We think of them as of a multiplicity of individual entities, in communication with one another, each one perhaps searching our world for his mortal twin. As the dawn advances and our windows grow palely bright (our bodies, too, reasserting their claims to selfhood), these visitors withdraw. Their chinks and chimes are stilled. Exchanging quick glances and enigmatic smiles, they retire once again into the forest of non-being. —Shall we ever, we wonder silently, confront them face to face?

Out over the bay (in our world) the sun has risen.

"IN A FIVE-MINUTE STILLNESS IN SEPTEMBER..."

In a five-minute stillness in September
the sunlight not yet departing from the goldenrod
that straggled down to shore's edge

it seemed all at once as if all might be understood—
if not articulately, at least in depth of heart—
by some less privileged life-form,

some being that would move, eat, procreate, and so on
but without the cutting edge of arrogance
that so disfigures our kind,

whose brain, pale instrument too fine for its data,
will, left to itself with nothing better to do,
multiply small distinctions

endlessly, uselessly in a tight compulsion
to impose its structure on the stuff of existence—
which indeed will bend itself

but only up to a certain unassayable point
beyond which, if the mind wander, it wanders untethered
from the glad solemn animal

cleaving to the heart of time, and holding in its own heart
as fulfillment of joy and pain (on days of September sun)
the certitude of being.

AFTER WEN CHENG-MING

At sunset the hills turn purple,
the trees are dripping still from afternoon rains.

One can sit alone in the long silence,
sit quietly and sing.

Best of all is having nothing to do:
let the world dispose of itself!

A narrow path leads up and around—
nearby, we know, is the home of an immortal.

AUTUMN MOMENTS

1

Tonight a smell of brown bread toasting
drifts from our kitchen down to the shore.
A damp breeze stirs as the tide recedes.

West of us, from the ruined dock,
children call out over the water
as one last lobsterman drones by.

It's growing cooler. Hand in hand
we gaze off oceanward beneath
a violet sky that darkens.

2

An old scraped board on the beach at Blue Hill,
pink for six minutes in the Autumn dawn,
abandoned, broken, unsecured—
reveals itself as everlasting.

3   (*York Village*)

In the quiet yard behind the Perkins House
this empty, chilly, bright October morning
marigolds glow against a weathered fence:

we hold life cleanly at our fingertips.

OCTOBER

October in Maine. The human touch:
outboards, power saws, and guns.
A landscape fading into death endures
the idiot stutterings, fatalistically.

I listen and I think. Where might be
a true New England emptied of the human?
Forest, lake unswerving through their changes
old as the ultimate earth, fresh as this dawn
and unwatched always but by one still man—
or man and woman, waiting quietly.

III   NEW YORK

THE BREATHING SPACE

I saw my dear one on the street
walking home with clothes in her arms—
clothes from the cleaners. She rippled along
past where the school was being built

on the next block. I called out to her,
shouting "Paula!" from my window:
shouted twice, three times. A black
construction worker grinned at me

from the unfinished rooftop. Paula
halted, turned and glanced about—
then, as I called her name once more,
looked up and smiled, and cried "I'm coming!"

Earlier that sharp Autumn day
we had phoned the small-town hospital
where an old brave friend lay slowly dying:
her voice slipped ghostlike down the wires...

It all gives way to death in the end—
this shifting show of shapes that pass:
that much comes clear as time moves on
and pains outmatch the early joy.

It all gives way in dreams that fade—
and what remains? a whiff, a trace,
some pale residuum of a life
changed now to dust and memory?

That's why I'm grateful for those times
when time itself comes to a stop
on some quite ordinary day,
comes to a stop for a random moment

in which the self gains breathing space
to find itself outside of time—
as I've been found, who still hold fast
that pause made radiant by her smile.

"I LOVE GRIM AUTUMN DAYS..."

I love grim Autumn days,
leaves falling yellow, brown
into the rainy gutters
along Fifth Avenue.

Life not so freely ventured
as in glad summertime
but durably maintained:
thus has my life found meaning.

Things yield their uttermost
only in death's conjunction—
I need not tell you this,
dear Paula, you who held
your dying brother's head.

Recall the legend, how
by the murderous ocean's rim
the maiden found, tossed up by the waves,
a simple key of gold—
the only one, it proved, designed to open
every locked door she'd meet with on her journey.

An answer may be given, it seems,
before the question's asked—
a pause outside of time precede
the immutable unwindings.
Death, too, is there with its meaning
before a life begins.

I walk the streets at duskfall
to the room we think of as timeless,
alert to the body's surge,
its doomed and bright defiance—
and climb a quiet staircase
to the mute, unchartered heaven
where lovers, freed from the great wheel,
may reassume their legends.

And so the Autumn deepens
till all the leaves are gone.
I hold you close, my dear one:
we lie in bliss together,
in modesty of silence—
while outside our dim window
the darkness settles down.

"I CALL IT BACK..."

I call it back, that cold midnight long past:
dark sky with cloud-shapes, here and there a star,
the air freezing my lungs. I wore no overcoat
as whistling to myself "Blues in the Night"
I crossed the chill quadrangles edged with snow.

I tried to see ahead. What would the years,
so darkly clouded, bring me? First, the war
with all its cruel rituals of loss—
the horror that had overhung my youth
full-blown at last and ready to devour.

But at its distant end, if I survived,
Might I not repossess the life I'd loved?
All ignorant, I thought it possible
and kept the hope clutched tightly through the long
disjunction and distress which I endured.

In vain, of course. The past is past retrieve,
and newer loves and griefs would intervene
dividing me from all I thought I'd known
until it seemed the boy of long ago
had been forsaken with his useless dreams...

But just last night, in the dark-lit restaurant,
as candles dimmed and you and I sat musing,
there in the gloom they played that tune again—
and I felt his presence, purged and strangely new,
in this long future suddenly at hand.

FIRST SNOW

You have gone your way,
        I'm going mine,
across this newly wakened city—
a city cleansed of memory
whose mutterings are stilled now by the whiteness.

It's separation...opening into chance.

I pause: my cheeks
        are bright and chilled.
A woman trudges past. "It's a blizzard!" she shouts.
People are skiing down Fifth Avenue.
Across from me, by the Engineers' Gate,
four laughing children build an enormous snowperson.
A car, half-buried, churns; its tires spin.
—I slog on through the glistening drifts.

At the end of this vast open day, I'm thinking,
when dusk descends and the lights are coming on,
and all is being gently folded in,
        patiently, in silence
our ways will reconverge...

I see it now—your brilliant smile of welcome.

WINTER POEM

We made love on a winter afternoon
and when we woke, hours had turned and changed,
the moon was shining, and the earth was new.
The city, with its lines and squares, was gone:
our room had placed itself on a small hill
surrounded by dark woods frosted in snow
and meadows where the flawless drifts lay deep.
No men there—some small animals all fur
stared gently at us with soft-shining eyes
as we stared back through the chill frosty panes.
Absolute cold gave us our warmth that night,
we held hands in the pure throes of delight,
the air we breathed was washed clean by the snow.

NEW YEAR'S POEM

January days, January days
chillingly on the move...

Early morning when all is still
I rest my forehead against the pane
(blanched with rime) and gaze far out
across the city's verticals
which all at once seem cleansed and true.

There's a whiter light in the air these days.
December's glooms have receded
with Christmas and its pangs of loss
as the planet takes a lifeward turn
and all at last is rebeginning...

Small clouds drift down the frozen sky.
Along the street rough children cluster, edging their way to school.
An eager jogger, puffy-breath'd, marks time before the stoplight.

New days, and time is on the move—
are we such as can match it?
Stick that old sign up over your bathtub, sweetheart—
the one that says MAKE IT NEW—
and I'll rig mine outside the shower stall.

It's January, the days are opening,
a moment's here to be seized—
and that old Yellow Emperor knew the score:
how life must be reshaped
day by ruthless day
unyieldingly to the end.

Begin. Right now.
We'll wash away the pities of the past
and march on with the days.

THE BUSSES

From our corner window
rainy winter mornings
we watch the yellow school busses
nudging their way down Park
moistly glowing, puddled by the rain.

Stopping at doorways here and there
where children climb aboard
they merge into the traffic's flow
and dwindle from our sight.

We watch—then turn away,
and when in changing light
we look again, we see a stream
dark and serene in China,
down which sleek goldfish dart and gleam.

THE DEPTHS

In watered wintry light,
the sleet now easing to rain,
we walk hand in hand, unspeaking,
the streets of this undersea city.

Turning the corner from Park
we have entered the untraveled block
where secretly, four flights above us,
a room and a bed await.

The bed, a strong four-poster
with polished spiral columns,
is Portuguese—carved in the old days
from rosewood, *pao santo*.

Mute in the shaded alcove
it takes note of our coming,
offering now as always
its benison of quiet

and its dreams—of Brazil,
of jungles and canopied tree-tops
through which the hot sun, thrusting down,
glints and scatters on dark-flowing rivers.

We sleep... and awake intertwined
in a room so beset by the dusk,
so peacefully severed from time,
that time itself seems to have altered—

and rise now, and cross to the window
where we stand gazing out through the mist.
Dear companion, we're up from the depths!—
our two sovereign selves reemerging
from all that dark splendor of passion.

THE MERMAID

A mermaid's out there, floating
this cool March day, above
soiled, square apartment blocks
I look southward upon...

Absurd! What chance these days
of such sweet revelations!
...Something, though, with breasts and
flowing hair is sunning herself

right here in our bright New York air
as though she'd just now surfaced
from everyone's unconscious.
Do you suppose she has, my dear,

a thing or two to tell us
of how she will protect those few
who visit her beneath the tides
but can't be coaxed to yield her name?

THE SMILE

"She walks in beauty," Byron wrote,
who knew the beauty of the real
in women's changes, and the play
of dark and bright their moods reveal.

He knew the sacred game. And I?
Along the way I'd learned it too,
but not its crowning elegance
until that April night with you.

I sat there in my chair, eyes closed,
waiting for the poem to come;
half-dozing, from my depths could hear
your movements in the adjoining room.

Opened my eyes a crack, and saw
you fixing flowers in our green vase:
African daisies fresh from Holland,
purple and red anemones.

Your hands were skilled. Your face, intent
upon that work you do so well,
took on a faint and far-off smile:
that smile told more than poems can tell

of beauty, and the grace of one
at home with her desires and powers.
I treasure it, and always shall—
that smile of yours above the flowers.

FIRST OF MAY

Through slats of our half-open shutters
I see green branches stirring
of lindens in hot sun
in the courtyard of St. Sergius' across the street.

Here in the blue studio
that strong light is subdued
as it angles in through the slats and across the bookshelves.
I have opened one window
and sit here in my usual chair
while sounds of spring come freely in from the street:
the screams of children playing ball
clop of ball on pavement
calls, complaints of mothers
squeak of delivery-bikes
bellowing of the old concierge at the Rumanian Embassy
who directs the parking of cars—
behind it all, the hustle of traffic going up and down Park.

Our indoor colors are rich in the afternoon glow.
On the chest your red-framed Picasso poster lies
waiting until we find the right precise spot for it.
Over the mantel Duke William's tapestry hangs tawny-bright.

I am thinking of a poem.
I am thinking also of making love to you
on our Portuguese bed, the moment you arrive.
Meanwhile, someone downstairs has begun cooking supper early
and even as I write, the light grows subtly cooler.

—It was not long ago—two weeks or a little more—
that on a chilly midnight
we awaited on this street
the procession to the Tomb:
those ancient bearded priests, those crucifers icons and banners
rounding the corner of the house built by the Chairman of the
        New York Central
passing through the court and up the outside stairs to the
        ballroom
which is now their chapel
and also, for one moment each year, the Tomb of Christ.

The knocking at the gate then. Empty! "He is risen."
The bearded one turns about in his blessed amazement
("Christos Basileus—Christ the King is risen!"
Defective loudspeakers gargle in Slavic gutturals)
and blesses us below.
The faithful cross themselves,
the cheap frame of light bulbs tacked up over the courtyard
flares out the miracle: Χβ

Easter. Faithful and faithless
we light our candles, we of the throng—
one by one, each from his neighbor—
to be held in one hand a few moments, the fire guarded in the
        curve of the other,
while the procession enters rejoicing
the Tomb that has opened, now, to a peopled heaven
where soon the chanting will begin.

I, as always,
take my flame from yours.

IV   THE SUMMIT

INTERIORLY

Interiorly
the space is opened
unto the god, unto the god it is said

as when I dreamed
of my grandmother standing
in the quiet room at the foot of the stairs

who had risen to greet me
and one other
(the late sun glowing through the long French window)

and who was that other
I knew not then
waking in my bed to the scent of verbena.

THREE CHILDREN LOOKING OVER THE EDGE OF THE WORLD

They came to the end of the road
and there was a wall across it
of cut stone—not very high.

Two of them boosted the third up
between them, he scrambled to the top
and found it wide enough to sit on easily.
Then he leaned back and gave the others a hand.

One two three in a row they sat there
staring: there was no bottom.
Below them a cliff went down and down for ever

and across from them, facing them, was nothing—
an emptiness that had no other side
and turned their vision back upon itself.

So there wasn't much to do or look at, after all.
One of them told a rhyme, the others chimed in,
and after a little while they swung around
and let themselves back down.

But when their feet touched solid road again
they saw at once they had dropped from the top of the sky
through sun and air and clouds and trees
and that the world was the wall.

THE SUMMIT

If you've just once been happy,
you have the right to assume
you're out of the reach of destruction.

I read that somewhere once and
didn't believe it at all
for happiness as I knew it was

only a point, quickly passed,
on the common road that leads
(as far as one can survey it) to

destruction and nowhere else.
What reasoning was this, which
would deny our time as we've lived it

and make us hostages to
assumptions no one has proved?
What can it possibly mean, to say

that those who once were happy
can "bear to die"? I wonder.
Why wouldn't it be all the harder

since they're asked to give up more?
It's those who are sick, wretched,
sunk in pain, who are ready to quit—

like my poor friend Costello,
at Hood back in '44,
who screamed so from his hospital bed

he burst a vein in his throat.
Destruction was fine by him...
But I've got the argument twisted—

I see it now all at once—
for plain willingness to die
isn't the point. The point is rather

whether, in someone's life, it
may come to pass that the self
reach a place of high vantage from which,

as from a mountain meadow,
future and past recede, and
the road itself lose its meaning. If

so, when the life is resumed,
something is left behind there
(wedded to the high place for ever)

which knows itself as lasting
beyond the self that moves on:
a thing at home in its happiness

as an oak tree is at home
in its own rich-textured shade,
or as an old fish deep in ocean

is at home, flexing his way
effortlessly, without thought...
And this thing it is which remains and

remembers itself and time
moving to their destruction
in the Self which they seek to rejoin.

ENVOI

Go, little book, and make your way
through the broad world as best you may.
I'll not be there to urge you on
or hold you back: you're on your own.

But you, dear Love, who've shared with me
time and events and history,
share now this simple dwelling-place
where timeless, we speak face to face.

ACKNOWLEDGMENTS

Many of the poems in this book first appeared (sometimes in earlier versions) in the following publications:

America
The American Scholar
Harper's
The Hudson Review
The Nation
New England Review
The New York Times
Paris Review
The Reaper
The Sewanee Review
The Southern Review

Grateful acknowledgment is made to the editors.

A NOTE ON THE AUTHOR

Frederick Morgan is a native New Yorker and graduate of Princeton University. During World War II he served in the Tank Destroyer Corps of the U.S. Army. A founder, in 1947 of *The Hudson Review*, he has directed it ever since, and is now co-editor of the magazine with his wife, the art and architecture critic Paula Deitz. His poems have appeared in a wide variety of magazines and journals in the United States and abroad. He has published ten books of poems, two collections of prose fables, and two books of translations. In 1984 he was named a Chevalier de l'Ordre des Arts et des Lettres by the government of France.

Morgan spends most of his time in New York City, with summers in Blue Hill, Maine.

7978